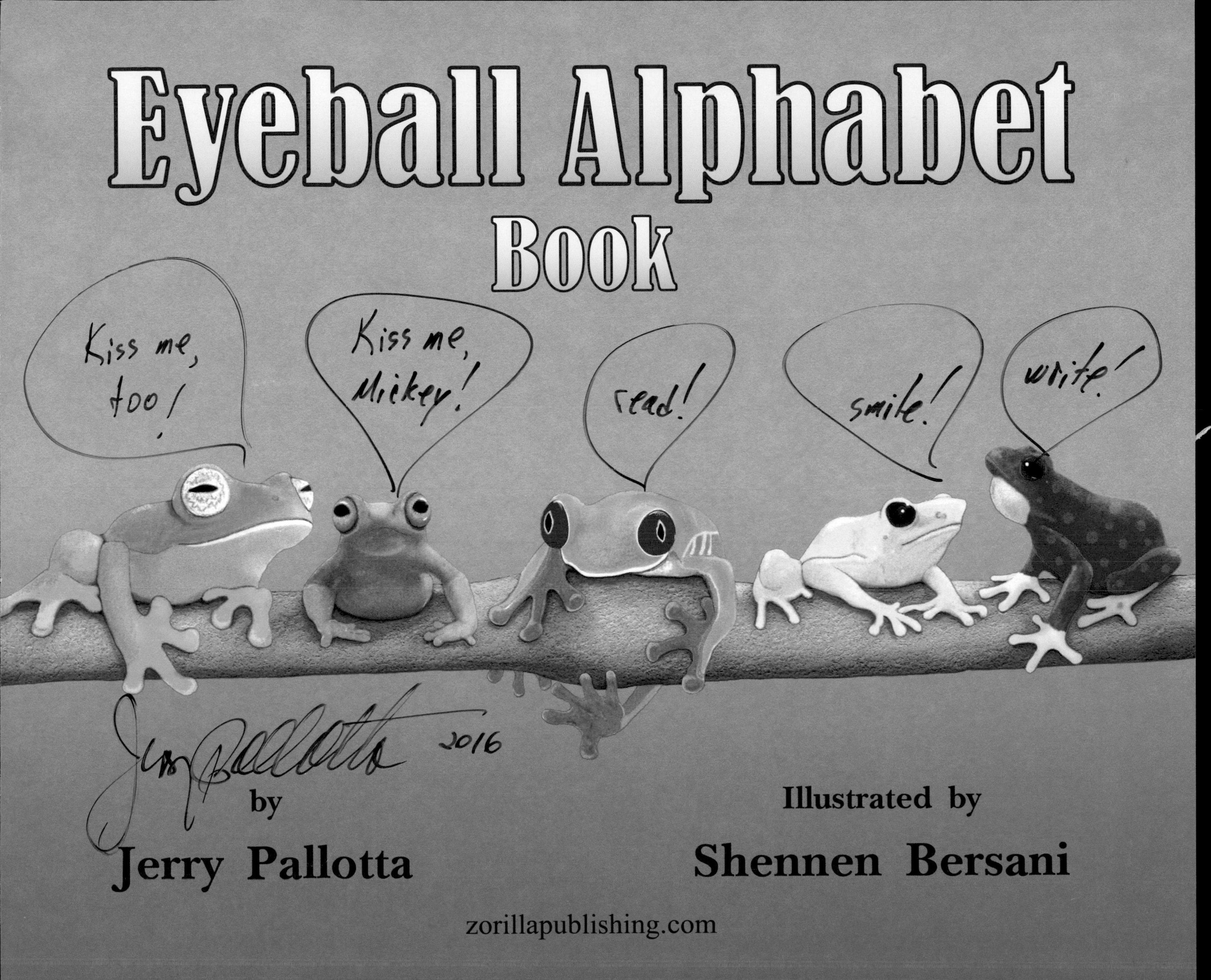
Eyeball Alphabet
Book
Kiss me, too!
Kiss me, Mickey!
read!
smile!
write!
Jerry Pallotta 2016
by
Jerry Pallotta
Illustrated by
Shennen Bersani
zorillapublishing.com

Dear Reader,

These eyeballs are looking at you. And guess what? Your eyeballs are looking at them. How do eyeballs work? In the *Eyeball Alphabet Book*, we are going to find out. Also look for *eye idioms* on every page. An idiom is an expression that means something different than what it might sound like.

To Katherine, Leigh, John and Jimmy Colihan.
— J.P.

To my daughter Karlene and son-in-law Patrick in honor of their big day, August 23.
— S.B.

ISBN 978-0-9863487-0-9

12 11 10 9 8 7 6 5 4 3 2 1 15 16 17 18 19 20/0

Printed in the U.S.A.

First hardcover printing, April 2015

A is for ***Alligator.*** The alligator has eyes that stick up out of the top of its head. It can look above the water while its head and body are hidden below water.

Aa

Keep your eye on the ball means to pay attention.

Bb

B is for ***Bay Scallop***. A bay scallop is a small clam. Look! It has lots of eyes. Blue eyes! The scallop's eyes help it locate food.

To have stars in your eyes means to be excited about the future and expect to become famous.

C is for ***Camel***. Human beings have one type of eyelid, which opens and closes. The camel has two types of movable eyelids. One clear eyelid goes from side to side. This allows the camel to see and protect its eyes while walking in a sandstorm. Another type of eyelid goes up and down and blocks light.

Cc

In the blink of an eye means something that happens fast.

Dd

D is for ***Dog***. This husky has one blue eye and one brown eye. In the animal kingdom, most creatures have eyes that are the same color. Think of your friends. Do you know anyone with one brown eye and one blue eye? Only six in 1,000 people have different-colored eyes.

To keep an eye out for something means to be alert and aware.

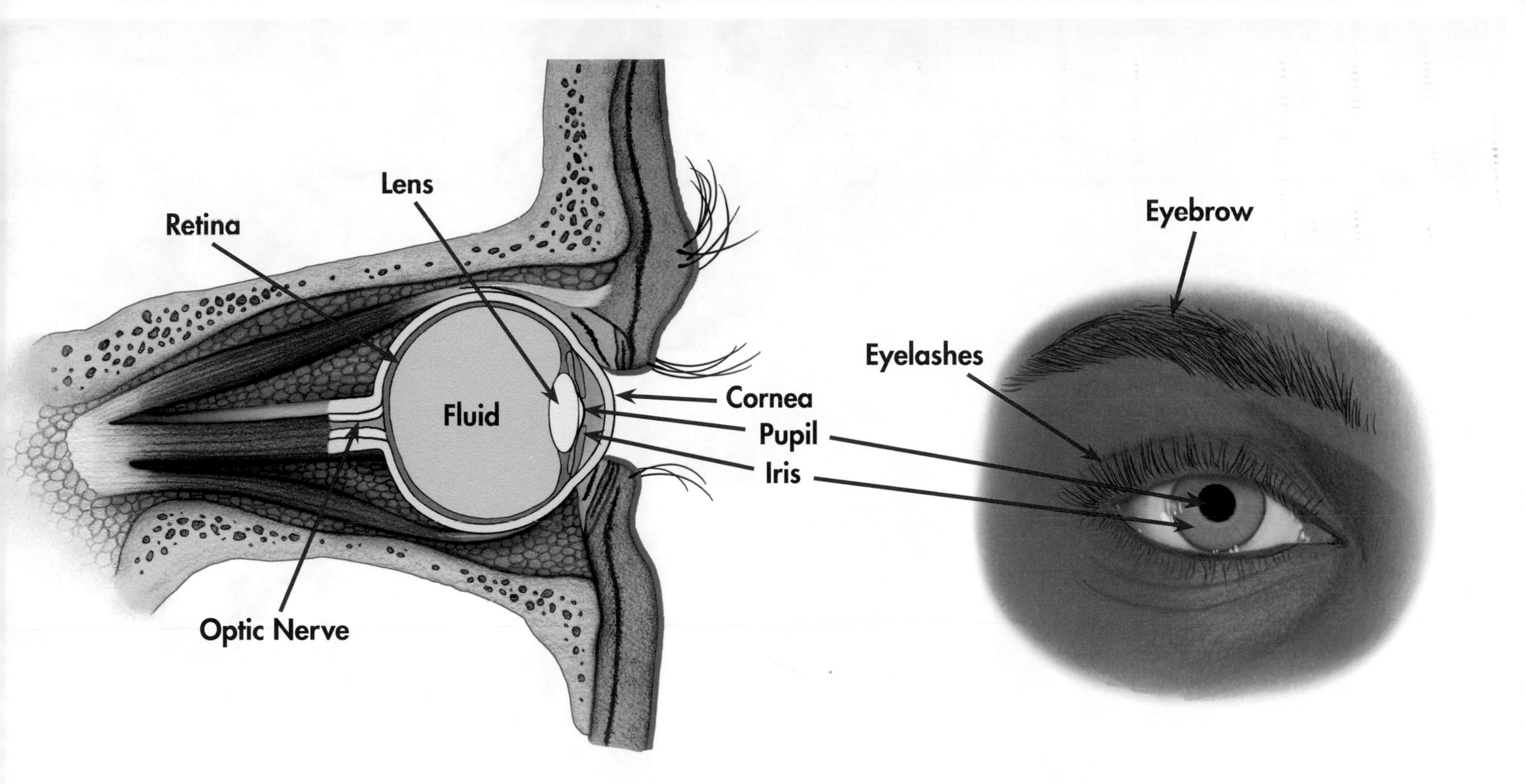

How does an eye work? First, you need light. Light reflects off the back of your eyeball, the retina. The retina converts the light into a signal. The signal is sent through the optic nerve to your brain. Your brain shows the image, and you can see!

To be a ***hawkeye*** means to be good at noticing things around you.

Ee

E is for ***Eel***. This eel's eyes are camouflaged. Its eyes look like the spots around them. Eels and most other fish do not have movable eyelids. Their eyes are always open.

The cleaner shrimp has blue eyes on short stalks. The stalks allow shrimp eyeballs to stick out.

In the eye of a storm means to be in the center of a difficult situation.

F is for ***Frog***. Eyes come in all different designs and colors. It doesn't matter what color your eyes are. It's how well you see that counts. Some animals' eye color might also be used to attract food or a mate.

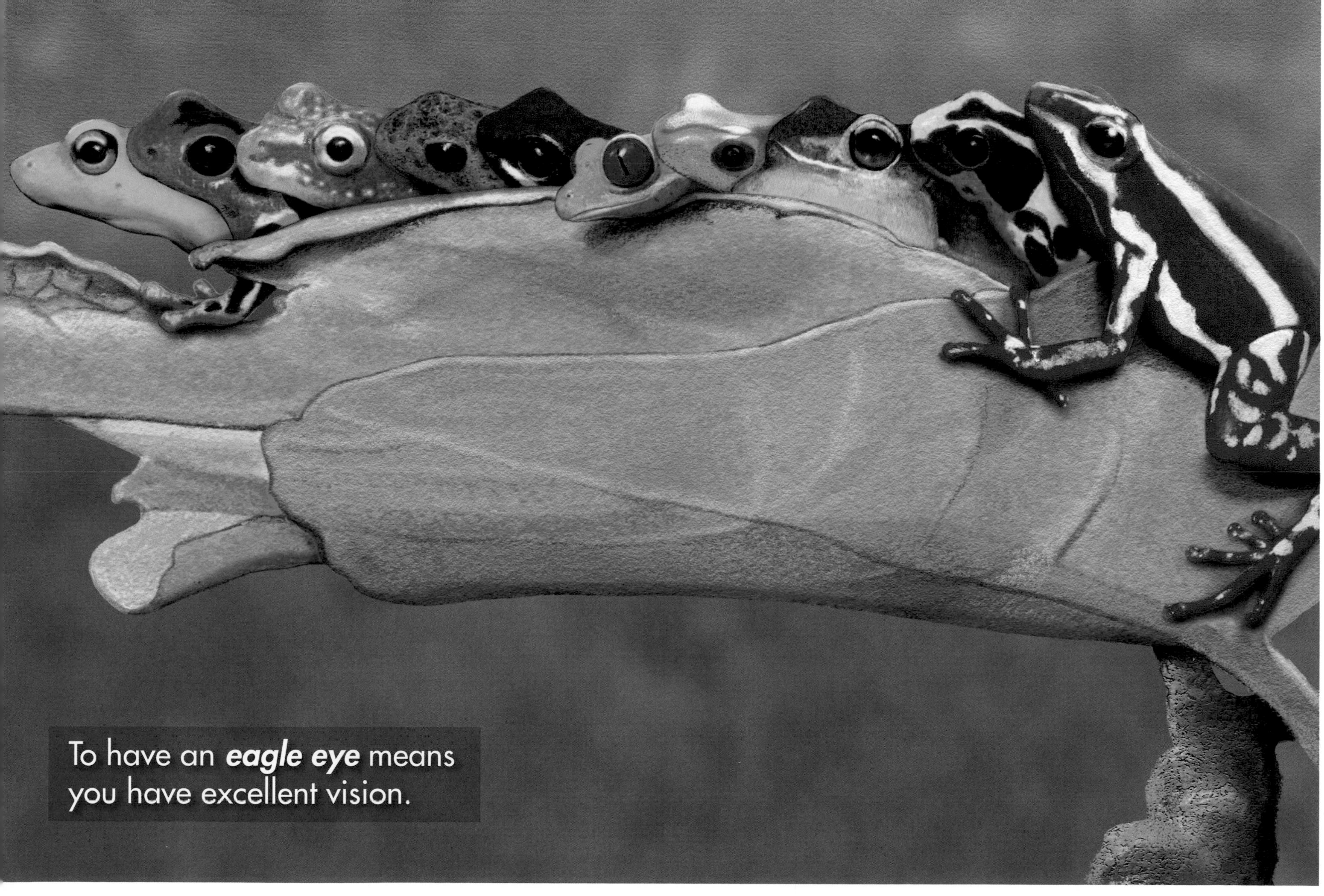

Ff

To have an ***eagle eye*** means you have excellent vision.

Ff

Just for fun, here is another F.

F is also for ***Fly.*** This is a common housefly. Flies are hard to catch because they have great eyesight. They have compound eyes. The red you see is not just one eye, but hundreds of individual eyes.

Swat! We missed again.

A sight for sore eyes means someone or something you are happy to see.

Gg

G is for ***Giant Squid***. The giant squid has the largest eyeball in the world. It is bigger than your head. It is about the size of a basketball. The huge eye allows it to see better in the deep, dark ocean where it lives.

To be in the public eye means to be known and talked about by many people.

Hh

Get some shut-eye means to get some sleep.

H is for ***Horse***. People have eyes with round pupils. A horse has eyes with oval-shaped pupils. A horse has monocular vision, which means each eye sees something different. A horse sees to either side, but not straight ahead.

When an animal's eyes are in front, it is called binocular vision. Each eye is looking at the same image. Binocular vision allows you to judge distance. This ability is called depth perception.

Ii

I is for ***Indri.*** The Indri is a lemur. In some cultures, people will not look a lemur in the eye. They may be afraid of the "evil eye."

To give someone the evil eye means to wish bad things will happen to them.

Jj

J is for ***Jaguar***. You are looking at a predator, which means an animal that hunts other animals. Here is a rhyme about predators: "Eyes in front, likes to hunt. Eyes on side, likes to hide." In other words, if an animal's eyes are in front, it usually is a predator. If an animal has eyes on the side, it usually is hunted by a predator. Humans have eyes in front.

To have eyes in the back of your head means to know everything that is going on around you.

Kk

K is for ***Kei Bat***. It's okay if a bat has poor eyesight. Most bats have big ears. Bats have sonar, which is a way to "see" with sound. The bat makes sounds and listens to the echoes. The echoes come back, giving the bat an image of what is around it.

To see eye to eye means to agree.

Ll

L is for ***Lobster***. Lobsters have eyes, but they do not have a brain. Without a brain, lobsters can't project an image. That's why lobsters can't see well. They notice only light and dark. Their antennae allow them to feel motion and vibrations in the water.

To turn a blind eye means to not care about something.

Mm

M is for ***Macaw***. Birds such as macaws can see better than humans can because they can see more kinds of light, such as ultraviolet light.

To do something with your eyes closed means you can perform the task really well.

Nn

N is for ***Night Crawler***. Night crawler is slang for earthworm. Earthworms have no eyes. They never need to visit an eye doctor! Learn the correct terms: An optometrist tests your vision. An optician fits you for glasses or contact lenses. An ophthalmologist is a doctor that specializes in eyes.

A ***private eye*** is slang for an undercover investigator.

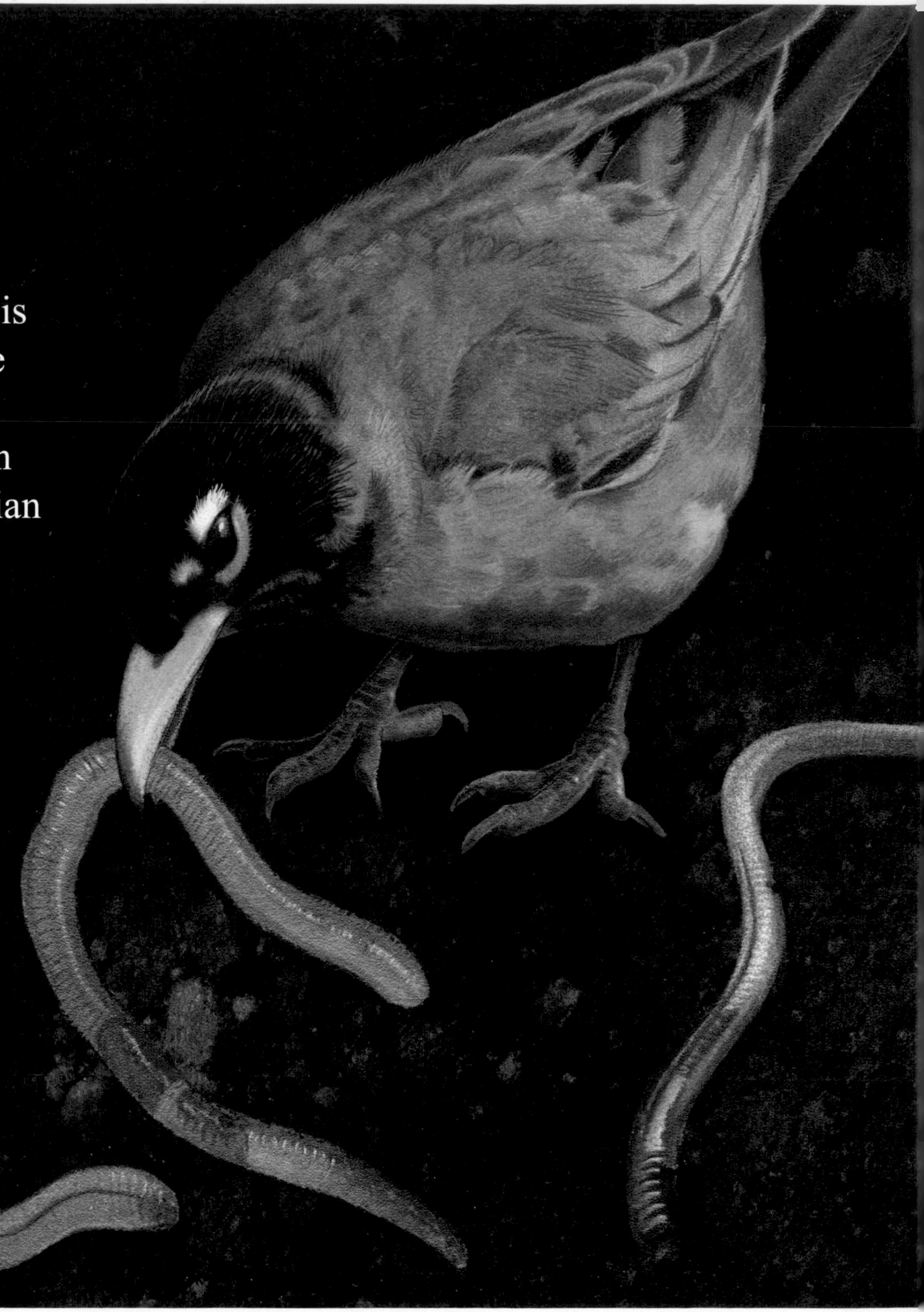

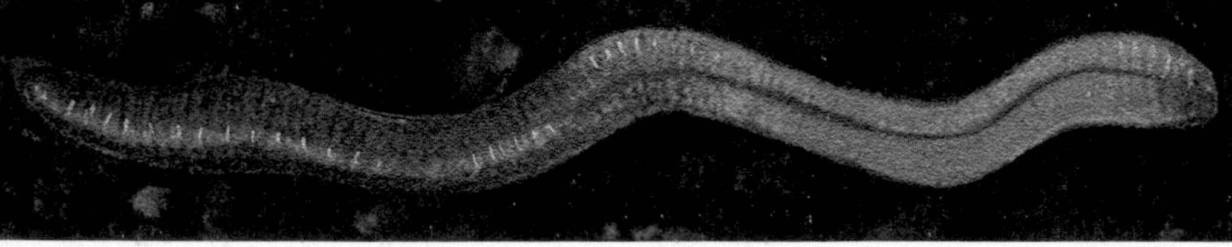

Oo

O is for ***Ostrich***.
It looks like this ostrich has healthy eyes. If an animal has trouble seeing things far away, it is called nearsighted. If it has trouble seeing things up close, it is farsighted. Kids who are nearsighted or farsighted can have their vision corrected with glasses or contact lenses. Having very low or no eyesight is called blindness.

Eye candy is a person or thing that is beautiful to look at.

Enjoy looking at these kooky glasses. Most glasses have lenses that help you see better.

Feast your eyes means to look at with pleasure.

P is for ***Python***. A python can see you not only with its eyes but also with its thermal sensors. It can "see" your heat. A thermal sensor is a different type of eye. A pit viper, another kind of snake, can also sense heat with its thermal sensors, known as "pits."

Pp

Without batting an eye means right away without thinking about it.

Qq

Q is for ***Quoll***. Marsupials are mammals with pouches. The quoll is a small marsupial. When a hungry hawk, python, or crocodile is hunting, a quoll may wish it had radar. But animals have no radar, which is an electronic tool that lets people see faraway objects.

To set your eyes on means to make a goal for yourself.

R is for ***Rhinoceros.*** A rhinoceros is the second-largest land mammal, but it has small eyes and poor eyesight. It makes up for its low vision with great hearing. Its ears can turn and listen in different directions.

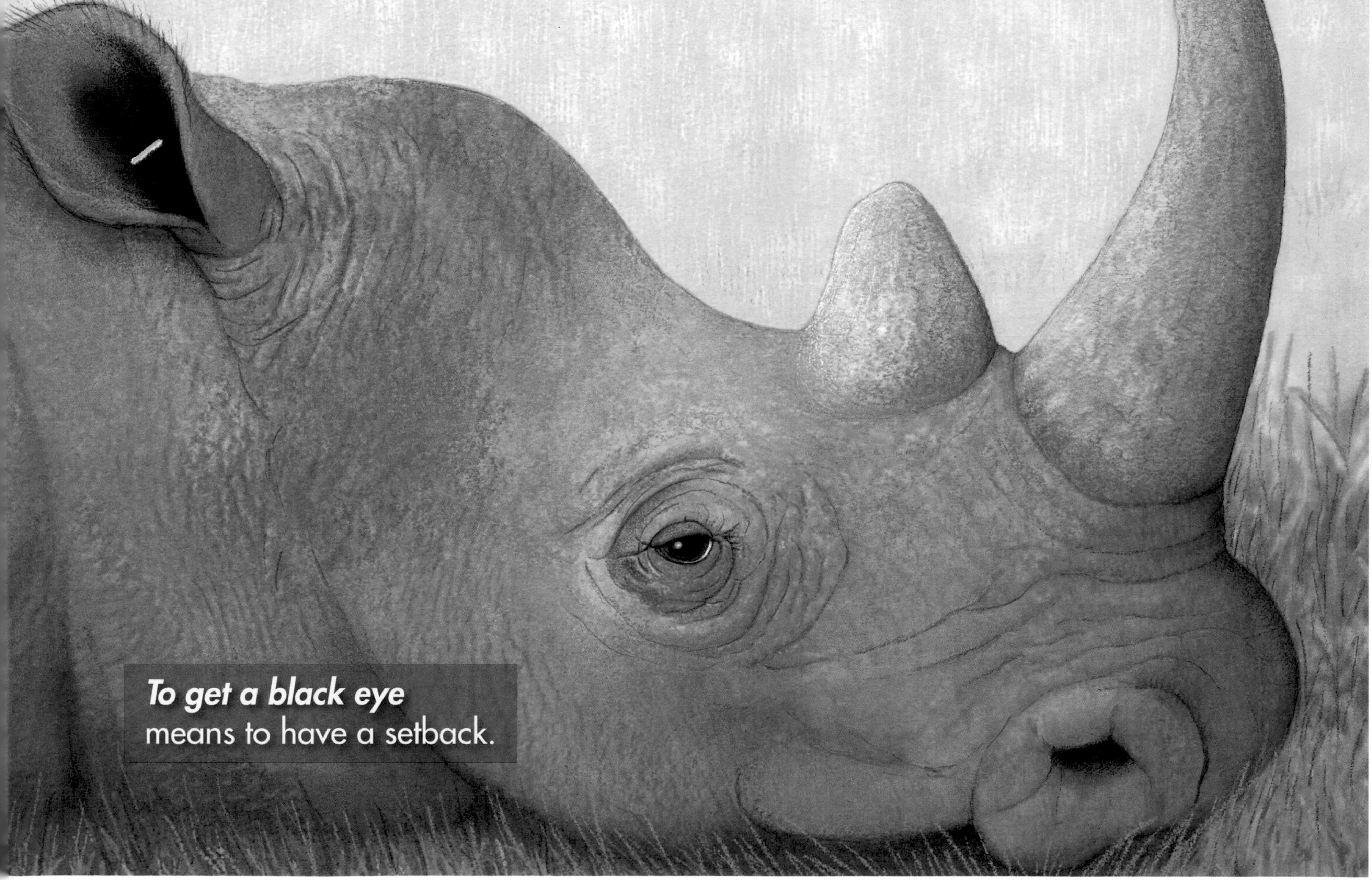

Rr

To get a black eye
means to have a setback.

Ss

S is for ***Spider***. Many kids know that spiders have eight legs. But did you also know that most spiders have eight eyes? Imagine a human being with eight eyes!

An eye for an eye means that if someone does something to you, you do the same to them. Not always a good idea!

Tt

T is for ***Tarsier***. It is holding a tarsier skull. Look how big the eye sockets are. This type of animal is rare. Each eye is bigger than its brain.

Apple of your eye
means your favorite.

Uu

U is for ***Uakari***. A uakari is a monkey. Its eyes are aligned, which means they are looking at the same object. Most eyes are aligned correctly. However, if a right eye looks left and a left eye looks right, this is called cross-eyed. If both eyes look outward, it is called walleyed.

A ***red-eye*** means to be tired or up all night.

Vv

V is for ***Vulture.*** Imagine being a bird, flying around and seeing everything from above. Some birds squeeze their eyes to sharpen their focus. Vultures can spot a dead mouse or a vole from far away.

Bird's-eye view means seen from above.

Ww

W is for ***Widemouth Blindcat.*** This fish lives in dark caves. It has no eyes. It doesn't need eyes, because there is no light. An olm, a jellyfish, a sea urchin, a blind salamander, a Mexican tetra, and a Yeti crab are other animals that have no eyes.

Eyes bigger than your stomach means you think you can eat more than you can.

Xx

X is for ***Xenosaur***. We used our eyes to search high and low for an animal that begins with the letter X. A xenosaur is from China. Its name sounds like a dinosaur, but it's a lizard.

A chameleon is a lizard that can move its eyes independently of each other.

Another pair of eyes means help from someone else when looking for something.

Yy

Y is for ***Yellow Fiddler Crab***. Its eyes are on long stalks. This crab can look all the way around. We call this 360-degree vision.

Pull the wool over their eyes means to fool someone.

Zz

Z is for ***Zebu***. A zebu is a type of cattle. This zebu has moths in its eyes that are drinking its tears. This doesn't bother the zebu.

To ***open your eyes*** means to become aware of something.

We end this book with a sheepdog. It can see you, but you can't see its eyes.

Take good care of your eyes!

- Wear protective equipment, such as safety goggles, for hobbies and sports.
- Avoid staring at really bright light, such as the sun.
- If something is in your eye, don't rub it.
- Get regular eye checkups.

We hope this book was an ***eye-opener***.